THE GOSPEL

AT 30,000
FEET

THE GOSPEL

AT 30,000
FEET

DIETER F. UCHTDORF

DESERET
BOOK

SALT LAKE CITY, UTAH

Library of Congress Cataloging-in-Publication Data

Names: Uchtdorf, Dieter F., author.
Title: The gospel at 30,000 feet / Dieter F. Uchtdorf.
Other titles: Gospel at thirty thousand feet
Description: Salt Lake City, Utah : Deseret Book, [2017] | Includes bibliographical references.
Identifiers: LCCN 2017040433 | ISBN 9781629723969 (hardbound : alk. paper)
Subjects: LCSH: Christian life—Mormon authors. | Mormons—Conduct of life. | The Church of Jesus Christ of Latter-day Saints—Doctrines. | Mormon Church—Doctrines.
Classification: LCC BX8656 .U2324 2017 | DDC 248.4/89332—dc23
LC record available at https://lccn.loc.gov/2017040433

Printed in the United States of America
Publishers Printing, Salt Lake City, UT

10   9   8   7   6   5   4   3   2

To Harriet,

the sunshine of my life

CONTENTS

PUBLISHER'S PREFACE

From the time President Dieter F. Uchtdorf first took the pulpit at general conference, members around the world have loved his stories about airplanes and the poignant gospel lessons he draws from them. In fact, his history of sharing tales of flight has led many listeners to find themselves internally asking a question as soon as he gets up to speak—the same question President Uchtdorf voiced one memorable conference: "What does it have to do with flying an airplane?"

Through the stories, lessons, and parables that have been gathered in this book, President Uchtdorf teaches readers exactly what every "it" has to do with flying an airplane—and what that has to do with the gospel of Jesus Christ. President Uchtdorf has made it clear over the years that if there is one thing he loves more than flying, it is the gospel that invites us to come unto Christ and be perfected in Him. President Uchtdorf's unique perspective as an Apostle of the Lord and one of the top pilots in the world provides an aerial view for us to chart the course the Lord would have us follow in our lives. His stories and analogies teach us about this journey of life, complete with lift, drag, turbulence, and guidance, as well as the joy we'll find in reaching our ultimate destination.

President Uchtdorf certainly knows something about trusting in the path the Lord has set out for us. From an early childhood in what was then Czechoslovakia, to his youth as a refugee in Germany, to his education and military experience that took him across the world, President Uchtdorf's course of life has not followed any straight and obvious line. But it is evident that the Lord's hand was guiding him every step of the way, preparing him to fulfill the roles coming to him—husband, father, pilot, Apostle.

It seems almost beyond probability that a young boy from Europe who was forced to flee his home more than once without any possessions in a dangerous, war-torn era would not simply survive but would find the gospel of Jesus Christ and grow up to become senior vice president and chief pilot of a major airline and Second Counselor in the First Presidency of The Church of Jesus Christ of Latter-day Saints. But President Uchtdorf's lifelong demonstration of the principles of lift, guidance, weathering turbulence, and reaching the destinations his Father in Heaven had planned for him have defied probability. His airplane stories teach powerful lessons, characterize his life of discipleship, and offer us guidance as we also strive to soar to our highest potential and navigate a life centered on and directed by Christ.

*Lufthansa Chief Pilot and Senior Vice President,
Flight Operations, 1982.*

PRINCIPLES OF FLIGHT

THE SAVIOR: THE WIND BENEATH OUR WINGS

During my professional life as an airline pilot, I sometimes had passengers visit the cockpit of my Boeing 747. They asked about the many switches, instruments, systems, and procedures and how all this technical equipment would help such a huge and beautiful airplane fly.

As with all pilots, I enjoyed the fact that they were impressed by the apparent complexity of this plane and that they wondered what kind of magnificent and brilliant person it takes to operate it! (At this point of my story, my wife and children would kindly interrupt and say with a twinkling in their eyes, "Pilots are born with a great measure of natural humility!")

To the visitors in my cockpit, I would explain that it takes a great aerodynamic design, many auxiliary systems and programs, and powerful engines to make this flying machine equal to the task of bringing comfort and safety to those joining the flight.

To simplify my explanation by focusing on the basics, I would add that all you really need is a strong forward thrust, a powerful upward lift, and the right aircraft attitude, and the laws of nature will carry the 747 and its passengers safely across continents and oceans, over high mountains and dangerous thunderstorms to its destination.

In recent years, I have often contemplated that being a member of The Church of Jesus Christ of Latter-day Saints invites us to ask similar questions. What are the basics, the fundamental principles of our membership in the kingdom of God on earth? After all is said and done, what will really carry us at times of greatest need to our desired eternal destination?

The Church, with all its organizational structure and programs, offers for its members many important activities aimed at helping families and individuals to serve God and each other. Sometimes, however, it can appear that these programs and activities are closer to the center of our heart and soul than the core doctrines and principles of the gospel. Procedures, programs, policies, and patterns of organization are helpful for our spiritual progress here on earth, but let's not forget that they are subject to change.

In contrast, the core of the gospel—the doctrine and the principles—will never change. Living according to the basic gospel principles will bring power, strength, and spiritual self-reliance into the lives of all Latter-day Saints.

To follow Christ is to become more like Him. It is to learn from His character. As spirit children of our Heavenly Father, we do have the potential to incorporate

Christlike attributes into our life and character. The Savior invites us to learn His gospel by living His teachings. To follow Him is to apply correct principles and then witness for ourselves the blessings that follow. This process is very complex and very simple at the same time. Ancient and modern prophets described it with three words: "Keep the commandments"—nothing more, nothing less.

By becoming more like the Savior, we will grow in our ability to "abound in hope, through the power of the Holy Ghost" (Rom. 15:13). We will "lay aside the things of this world, and seek for the things of a better" (D&C 25:10).

This leads me back to my aerodynamic analogy from the beginning. I spoke of focusing on the basics. Christlike attributes are the basics. They are the fundamental principles that will create "the wind beneath our wings." As we develop Christlike attributes in our own lives, step-by-step, they will "bear [us] up as on eagles' wings" (D&C 124:18).

In the cockpit of a B-747.

Our faith in Jesus Christ will provide power and a strong forward thrust; our unwavering and active hope will provide a powerful upward lift. Both faith and hope will carry us across oceans of temptations, over mountains of afflictions, and bring us safely back to our eternal home and destination.

LIFT

TAKING FLIGHT

On December 17, 1903, a dream of mankind was fulfilled as Wilbur and Orville Wright made the first controlled, powered flight. The distance was about 120 feet, or 37 meters—about half the length of a 747 jumbo jet—and the duration was about twelve seconds. That's shorter than the time it takes me to climb the stairs leading up to the 747 cockpit. By today's standards, it was a very short flight, but at that time it was an accomplishment that few believed would ever be possible.

Wilbur and Orville had parents who encouraged education, religion, and family values. Both brothers had their share of serious illnesses. They went through difficult times of trouble, perplexity, and even despair, wondering if they would ever succeed. They tried different vocations as printers, bicycle repairmen, bicycle manufacturers, and, eventually, aircraft inventors. Throughout their lives, whenever they picked a project to work on, they were focused and worked as a team.

The Wright brothers committed themselves to do what no one else had ever done before. They took time to do their homework. They were humble and smart enough to appreciate and learn about the work of others who went before. And they tackled the problem line upon line, precept upon precept. They realized that there were three main requirements for a practical flying machine: first, the pilot had to be able to *control the aircraft*; second, the wings had to *produce lift*; third, it had to be *powered by an engine* to stay aloft.[1]

They had their goals defined and worked diligently on them one day at a time. Leonardo da Vinci said, "He turns not back who is bound to a star."[2]

Similar principles and requirements apply to your own journey through life and toward the destination of eternal life. Divine principles have to be learned and lived as you prepare to rise up on the wings of eagles.

FIRST: YOU HAVE TO LEARN TO CONTROL YOURSELF

It isn't until you come to a spiritual understanding of who you are that you can begin to take control of yourself. As you learn to control yourself, you will get control of your life. If you want to move the world, you first have to move yourself.

PRESIDENT SPENCER W. KIMBALL (1895–1985)
OFTEN QUOTED AN UNKNOWN AUTHOR:

"The greatest battle of life is fought out within the silent chambers of the soul. A victory on the inside of a man's heart is worth a hundred conquests on the battlefields of life. To be master of yourself is the best guarantee that you will be master of the situation. Know thyself. The crown of character is self-control."[3]

Be responsive to the counsel of the prophets, seers, and revelators, who will help you to reach true self-mastery. Be responsive to the promptings of the Spirit. The Spirit will influence your conscience and help you to refine yourself by working on the little tasks of self-control—like controlling your thoughts, words, and actions—which lead to self-control of your whole self, of mind, body, and spirit. Remember, *anger* is only one letter short of *danger*.

Your choices are the mirror of your self-control. They will lead you to your eternal destination if they are made with divine direction and control. Stay morally clean. Keep a clean mind and heart. Your thoughts will determine your actions. Control your thoughts. Don't submit yourself to temptation. Aristotle said, "For where it is in our power to act it is also in our power not to act."[4]

Control wisely and select carefully what you will invite via a mouse click or remote control into your home or office. Select reading material, movies, TV shows, and any other form of entertainment that bring good, uplifting thoughts rather than unwholesome desires.

SECOND: YOUR ATTITUDE WILL DETERMINE YOUR LIFT AND ALTITUDE

The Wright brothers knew that in addition to keeping control of the aircraft, they needed to produce enough lift to keep their flying machine aloft. Dictionaries describe *lift* as something like the following: to carry or direct from a lower to a higher position; the power or force available for raising to a new level or altitude; a force acting in an upward direction, opposing the pull of gravity.

The Psalmist sets the sights even higher: "Unto thee, O Lord, do I lift up my soul" (Ps. 25:1) and "I will lift up mine eyes unto the hills, from whence cometh my help" (Ps. 121:1). HE INVITES YOU TO FLY WITH THE EAGLES, NOT TO SCRATCH WITH THE CHICKENS.

Lifting your eyes toward the God of heaven is a process of cultivating your own very personal spirituality. It is a desire to live in harmony with the Father; the Son, our Savior; and the Holy Ghost. It is also your ability to be truly "submissive, meek, humble, patient, full of love, willing to submit to all things which the Lord seeth fit to inflict upon [you], even as a child doth submit to his father" (Mosiah 3:19).

Sincere prayer. With the right attitude—which, incidentally, is also needed to produce sufficient lift for an airplane—you will be able to effectively communicate with your Heavenly Father and not to just say your prayers. You will be able to say prayers that will go beyond the ceiling of the room, prayers not filled with trite repetitions or spoken without thinking but filled with your deep yearning to be one with your Father in Heaven.

Prayer, if given in faith, is acceptable to God at all times. If you ever feel you cannot pray, that is the time when you definitely need to pray. Nephi taught in plainness, "If ye would hearken unto the Spirit [of God] which teacheth a man to pray, ye would know that ye must pray; for the evil spirit . . . teacheth him that he must not pray" (2 Ne. 32:8).

Obedience assures us an answer to our prayers. We read in the New

Testament, "And whatsoever we ask, we receive of him, because we keep his commandments, and do those things that are pleasing in his sight" (1 John 3:22).

The Prophet Joseph Smith learned in a revelation given to him in Kirtland in 1831, "He that asketh in the Spirit asketh according to the will of God; wherefore it is done even as he asketh" (D&C 46:30).

In order to lift, enhance, and cultivate your relationship with God as His spiritual children, you have the unique opportunity to converse with the supreme source of wisdom and compassion in the universe.

Simple but sincere and mighty prayers offered daily will help you lift your lives to a higher spiritual altitude. In your prayers you praise God, give thanks to Him, confess weaknesses, petition needs, express deep devotion to your Heavenly Father, and then trust in Him and in His timing. As you do this in the name of Jesus Christ, the Redeemer, you perform a spiritual effort that leads to increased inspiration, revelation, and righteousness—not self-righteousness—and brings the brightness of heaven into your lives.

Opposition and agency. A word of caution: in aerodynamics, gravity and drag work in *opposition* to lift. This same important principle has been an integral part of the plan of salvation from the beginning. As Lehi explained, "For it must needs be, that there is an *opposition* in all things" (2 Ne. 2:11; emphasis added). And as the angel taught King Benjamin, "For the natural man is an enemy to God . . . *unless* he yields to the enticings of the Holy Spirit" (Mosiah 3:19; emphasis added).

This leads us to God's great gift to His children: agency.

Lehi taught this most important doctrine to his children. He said: "The Lord God gave unto man that he should act for himself. . . . And they are free to choose liberty and eternal life, through the great Mediator of all men, or to choose captivity and death, according to the captivity and power of the devil; for he seeketh that all men might be miserable like unto himself" (2 Ne. 2:16, 27).

You have agency, and you are free to choose. But there is actually no free agency. Agency has its price. You have to pay the consequences of your choices.

Human agency was purchased with the price of Christ's suffering. The power of Christ's Atonement overcomes the effect of sin on the condition of wholehearted repentance. Through and by the Savior's universal and infinite Atonement, all have been redeemed from the Fall and have become free forever to act for themselves (see 2 Ne. 2:26).

Agency is a spiritual matter. Without awareness of alternatives, you could not choose. Agency is so important in your lives that you not only *can* choose obedience or rebellion, but you *must*. During this life you cannot remain on neutral ground; you cannot abstain from either receiving or rejecting the light from God.

By learning to use the gift of agency to make right decisions, you will increase your spiritual lift and altitude. You will also quickly recognize one other prime source of spiritual truth: the written word of God.

Feasting on the word. Lifting your eyes toward heaven requires an attitude directed upward. With this positive attitude toward life comes the desire to *feast* "upon the word of Christ" (2 Ne. 31:20), not to just occasionally nibble on the scriptures or the words of the prophets.

Feasting includes searching, pondering, asking, praying, and living the word of God. Read the holy scriptures as if they were written for you—for they are. Nephi said, "For behold, the words of Christ will tell you all things what ye should do" (2 Ne. 32:3).

One powerful scripture in the New Testament, James 1:5, initiated a wonderful process that led to the Restoration of all things. May I ask you to take time to feast upon the word of God? It is available twenty-four hours a day, seven days a week, but should not be treated like a fast-food service. Jesus asked listeners to go home and ponder what He had taught them (see 3 Ne. 17:3). This pondering, feasting, and meditating will help you "know to what source [you] may look for a remission of [your] sins" (2 Ne. 25:26).

Praying and feasting upon the word of God are two elements of a heavenward attitude that will also enhance your work ethic and your willingness to serve and lift others. It will help you to carry Church responsibilities with the willingness to magnify your callings without trying to magnify yourself. With this divine attitude you will be more concerned about *how* you serve rather than *where* you serve.

King Benjamin taught, "I tell you these things that ye may learn wisdom; that ye may learn that when ye are in the service of your fellow beings ye are only in the service of your God" (Mosiah 2:17). And we do this by "lift[ing] up the hands which hang down" (Heb. 12:12).

THIRD: YOU NEED TO FIND AND TRUST THE
TRUE SOURCE OF DIVINE POWER

The Wright brothers needed engine power to make the airplane fly. Without it there would have been no lift, no forward motion to enable flight—no airplane.

You have an all-encompassing true source of power available to help you reach the purpose of your creation. This is the power of God exercising a subtle and loving influence in the lives of His children, lifting you and keeping you aloft. It is manifested as the Light of Christ, the Spirit of Christ, the Spirit of God, the Holy Ghost, and the gift of the Holy Ghost.

The Latin source of the word **COMFORTER**— *com fortis*—means "**TOGETHER STRONG**." As the Holy Ghost visits your own spirit, you become stronger than you are by yourself. When you receive the Holy Ghost, you receive strength, power, peace, and comfort.

Elder Parley P. Pratt (1807–57) of the Quorum of the Twelve Apostles stated that the Holy Ghost "inspires virtue, kindness, goodness, tenderness, gentleness and charity. It develops beauty of person, form and features. It tends to health, vigor, animation and social feeling. It develops and invigorates all the faculties of the physical and intellectual man. It strengthens, invigorates and gives tone to the nerves. In short, it is . . . marrow to the bone, joy to the heart, light to the eyes, music to the ears, and life to the whole being."[5]

President Marion G. Romney (1897–1988), First Counselor in the First Presidency, gave us encouragement: "You can make every decision in your life correctly if you can learn to follow the guidance of the Holy Spirit. This you can do if you will discipline yourself to yield your own feelings to the promptings of the Spirit. Study your problems and prayerfully make a decision. Then take that decision and say to him, in simple, honest supplication, 'Father, I want to make the right decision. I want to do the right thing. This is what I think I should do; let me know if it is the right course.' Doing this, you can get the burning in your bosom, if your decision is right. . . . When you learn to walk by the Spirit, you never need to make a [wrong decision]."[6]

The Prophet Joseph Smith talked about the promptings of the Spirit as "sudden strokes of ideas."[7]

The Holy Ghost will make you independent. If you will learn how to have the Holy Ghost as a constant companion, all other needful things will fall in place. Through your personal righteousness the Spirit of God will guide you to learn to control yourself, to enhance your attitude, to increase your spiritual altitude, and to find and trust the true source of divine power.

THE WIND BENEATH YOUR WINGS

Many things are required to make an airplane fly and fly safely, but the most important thing, as I used to call it, is the "wind beneath your wings." Without it, there is no lift, no climb, no flight into the wild blue yonder or to faraway, beautiful destinations.

The Holy Ghost will be the wind beneath your wings, placing in your hearts the firm conviction of the divinity of the Lord Jesus Christ and His place in the eternal plan of God your Eternal Father. Through the Holy Ghost you will know *your* place in this plan and *your* divine eternal destination. You will be converted to the Lord, His gospel, and His Church, and you will never fall away.

CREATING LIFT

One of the things I loved about flying as an airline pilot in a European weather environment was departing from a dark and rainy airport, climbing through thick and threatening clouds, and then suddenly breaking through the dark mist, steeply gaining altitude into the bright sunshine and into the endless blue sky. It almost felt like being pulled up into a new and pristine sphere. These precious moments were the prize won for getting up early and not shying away from a rain-dripping airplane as I did my preflight walk-around.

I often marveled at how this physical act parallels our personal lives. How often do we find ourselves surrounded by threatening clouds and stormy weather, wondering if the darkness will ever pass? If there were only a way for us to lift ourselves up from the turmoil of life and break through to a place of peace and calm.

Members of The Church of Jesus Christ of Latter-day Saints know that such a thing is possible; there is a way to rise above the turbulence of everyday life.

The knowledge, understanding, and guidance we receive from the word of God and from prophetic guidance in our day show us how to do exactly that.

In order to get an airplane off the ground, you must create lift. In aerodynamics, lift happens when air passes over the wings of an airplane in such a way that the pressure underneath the wing is greater than the pressure above the wing. When the upward lift exceeds the downward pull of gravity, the plane rises from the ground and achieves flight.

In a similar way, we can create lift in our spiritual life.

WHEN THE FORCE THAT IS PUSHING US HEAVENWARD IS GREATER THAN THE TEMPTATIONS AND DISTRESS THAT DRAG US DOWNWARD, WE CAN ASCEND AND SOAR INTO THE REALM OF THE SPIRIT.

I think back on my days as a pilot and those times when thick clouds and threatening thunderstorms made all appear dark and gloomy. In spite of how bleak things looked from my earthly vantage point, I knew that above the clouds the sun beamed brightly like a dazzling jewel in an ocean of blue skies. I did not have faith that such was the case—I *knew* it. I knew it because I had experienced it for myself. I did not need to rely on other people's theories or beliefs. I knew.

In the same way that aerodynamic lift can transport us above the outer storms of the world, I know that the principles of spiritual lift can take us above the inner storms of life.

And I know something else. Although it was a breathtaking experience to break through the clouds and fly to the bright blue horizon, that is nothing compared to the wonders of what we all can experience as we lift up our hearts in humble and earnest prayer.

Prayer helps us transcend the stormy times. It gives us a glimpse of that blue sky that we cannot see from our earthly vantage point, and it reveals to us another vista—a glorious spiritual horizon filled with hope and the assurance of the bright blessings the Lord has promised to those who love and follow Him.

GUIDANCE ON THE JOURNEY

DIRECTED BY THE LORD

On one occasion, my profession as a B-747 captain took me home on a flight from Dallas, Texas, to Frankfurt, Germany. I had just attended general conference of The Church of Jesus Christ of Latter-day Saints as a General Authority. Now I was heading home while working in my profession I loved so much. One flight attendant asked if a few passengers could take a peek into the cockpit. When they entered, they explained that they too had attended general conference and were now surprised to have a General Authority fly them home to Germany. We greeted each other happily and were grateful for the pleasant coincidence in our travel plans.

As the flight progressed, the day turned into a moonless night, and myriads of stars covered the sky. I contemplated this awesome sight from the cockpit, and my thoughts went back to the many miracles I have seen in my life.

One occurred many years ago, shortly after the horrors of the Second World War. I was baptized at age eight in Zwickau, Sachsen, in eastern Germany. It came about because of Sister Ewig, a white-haired, courageous, and caring lady who shared the restored gospel of Jesus Christ with my grandmother and parents, and they did not hesitate to accept the challenge to follow the promptings of the Spirit and accept a new religion. How I love them for that! In 1952 my family had to leave that part of my homeland, expecting never to see it again. We went to Frankfurt, where I was ordained a deacon and taught by tough but loving Church leaders to appreciate the value of work and service.

At the same time, in the heart of western Germany, another marvelous lady, recently widowed, still in her thirties, was terrified by the unbearable difficulties of the future. She had two young daughters and felt alone in her disheartening circumstances and in a country without hope. In her time of deep distress, two young missionaries rang the doorbell and brought the message of light, truth, and hope—and she accepted.

I give thanks eternally to Sister Ewig, to those diligent American missionaries, and to Sister Carmen Reich—who became my mother-in-law—for their faith, strength, courage, and willingness to listen to the still, small voice. My life has been very different because of the miraculous insight of these great individuals.

In the early fifties, many Saints left Europe to go to Zion. But then the Brethren reminded us that Zion could be anywhere around the globe if the pure in heart were willing to establish it. The Saints had faith and many stayed, and Zion increased in beauty and holiness. Stakes were organized and strengthened. Nevertheless, Germany still had two completely different political systems divided by concrete-walled boundaries.

During these dreadful years, my dear wife, Harriet, encouraged me never to lose hope that someday there would be one Germany again. How grateful I am for her, her love and partnership, and for our family.

In 1976, President Monson gave my country a blessing with promises far beyond logical or political reasoning. It was a prophetic promise which required modern-day miracles. And the miracles occurred.

In 1989, the Berlin Wall fell, and about a year later, Germany was reunited. The borders were enlarged, and Zion was enabled to put on her beautiful garments—there are now two temples in Germany, soon to be fourteen temples in Europe, and more to come. The kingdom of God is expanding rapidly into all parts of the world—even moving far beyond the geographic or political boundaries of yesterday. Missionaries are now serving in places most of us have to look up in dictionaries or cannot find easily on maps.

Truly these are modern miracles.

Now back to that dark night over the North Atlantic. As we were safely directing our big jet to its destination, we had to be extremely careful and precise in entering the geographic coordinates into the navigation reference system. The navigation system relied on the information we had entered even before we had started our flight. This information had to be true and valid because it was the foundation for all future course decisions.

THE GOSPEL OF JESUS CHRIST IS THE ONLY TRUE AND VALID BASIS FOR OUR LIVES.

If we enter its values into our system—into "all [our] heart, might, mind and strength" (D&C 4:2)—we will know how to choose and follow the course back to our heavenly home.

On long-range flights, shortwave radio frequencies are still used to coordinate conflicting traffic. These frequencies are often crowded, and static distorts the messages. The same is true for our lives. Everybody wants to get their often conflicting messages across. We have to train and condition ourselves to hear the still, small voice, never to be distracted or to stop listening because of too much static on that sacred frequency. This can best be done by internalizing and acting according to the moral and ethical standards we receive from the scriptures and the living prophets.

From the Prophet Joseph Smith to our living prophet today, we are receiving updated sacred guidance according to our needs and readiness. The general conference messages by our prophets, seers, and revelators are given to us by the Lord in His own time, in His own way, and for a very special purpose.

JESUS CHRIST, THE SON OF GOD, IS THE SOURCE AND FOUNDATION OF OUR COURSE THROUGH LIFE. HIS MESSAGE MAY BE STILL, BUT IT IS CLEAR AND WILL REACH OUR HEARTS. HIS MESSAGE IS THE GOSPEL OF JOY, HOPE, COURAGE, TRUTH, LOVE, AND OF MIRACLES.

HEAVENLY FATHER'S
FLIGHT PLAN

In my profession as an airline captain, one of my routes was from Frankfurt, Germany, to Miami, Florida. On one flight, we had completed our departure out of Europe and were on our assigned route for an orderly and safe crossing of the North Atlantic. Our Boeing 747 was cruising smoothly at 33,000 feet. Behind us lay the green coast of Ireland, and only four hours ahead was Newfoundland, on the east coast of the North American continent. The planned flight time from Frankfurt to Miami was ten hours, sixteen minutes, and we would cover 4,955 nautical miles. The weather forecast called for an uneventful flight. We had 386 passengers aboard.

While checking the instruments and communicating by shortwave radio with ground control, we saw the contrails of two other jetliners many miles ahead. Obviously, we were faster, and soon we were close enough to recognize the aircraft types and their markings. They were on the same North Atlantic crossing route. One was 2,000 feet above us, and the other was 2,000 feet below our cruising level. As we slowly overtook those beautiful aircraft, my copilot mentioned how remarkable it was that because of true and accurate information entered into the navigation units at the start of our flights and as we progressed, all three jets were on precisely the same track, separated only by altitude. And we would continue to be so, if the crews used identical navigational information leading to the same destination.

As I have contemplated the truth of this statement and its application to our lives, I have arrived at a question: Do we all know our destination? Are we on the right track, and are we continuously feeding our spiritual navigation system with light and truth? It is imperative for a pilot to know the destination before submitting a flight plan. Heavenly Father has prepared a flight plan for us that will lead us back to Him. We read in the Pearl of Great Price, "For behold, this is my work and my glory—to bring to pass the immortality and eternal life of man" (Moses 1:39). It is a plan for our happiness.

The gospel of Jesus Christ provides the true and accurate information by which to direct our lives. If we let it enter into our system—into our hearts and minds—we will know who we are, where we came from, why we are here, and what we need to do to reach again our final destination—our heavenly home.

SIMPLICITY

There is a beauty and clarity that comes from simplicity that we sometimes do not appreciate in our thirst for intricate solutions.

For example, it wasn't long after astronauts and cosmonauts orbited the earth that they realized ballpoint pens would not work in space. And so some very smart people went to work solving the problem. It took thousands of hours and millions of dollars, but in the end, they developed a pen that could write anywhere, in any temperature, and on nearly any surface. But how did the astronauts and cosmonauts get along until the problem was solved? They simply used a pencil.

Leonardo da Vinci is quoted as saying that "simplicity is the ultimate sophistication."[1] When we look at the foundational principles of the plan of happiness, the plan of salvation, we can recognize and appreciate in its plainness and simplicity the elegance and beauty of our Heavenly Father's wisdom. Then, turning our ways to His ways is the beginning of our wisdom.

TRUST AND FAITH

The purpose of faith is not to change God's will but to empower us to act on God's will. Faith is trust—trust that God sees what we cannot and that He knows what we do not (see Isa. 55:8–9). Sometimes, trusting our own vision and judgment is not enough.

I learned this as an airline pilot on days when I had to fly into thick fog or clouds and could see only a few feet ahead. I had to rely on the instruments that told me where I was and where I was headed. I had to listen to the voice of air traffic control. I had to follow the guidance of someone with more accurate information than I had. Someone whom I could not see but whom I had learned to trust. Someone who could see what I could not. I had to trust and act accordingly to arrive safely at my destination.

Faith means that we trust not only in God's wisdom but that we trust also in His love. It means trusting that God loves us perfectly, that everything He does—every blessing He gives and every blessing He, for a time, withholds—is for our eternal happiness (see 2 Ne. 26:24).

LIGHT AND TRUTH

As an airline pilot, I flew numerous hours across continents and oceans during the darkness of night. Watching the night sky out of my cockpit window, especially the Milky Way, often made me marvel at the vastness and depth of God's creations—what the scriptures describe as "worlds without number" (Moses 1:33).

It was less than a century ago that most astronomers assumed that our Milky Way galaxy was the only galaxy in the universe.[1] They supposed all that lay beyond our galaxy was an immense nothingness, an infinite void—empty, cold, and devoid of stars, light, and life.

As telescopes became more sophisticated—including telescopes that could be launched into space—astronomers began to grasp a spectacular, almost incomprehensible truth: the universe is mind-bogglingly bigger than anyone had previously believed, and the heavens are filled with numberless galaxies, unimaginably far away from us, each containing hundreds of billions of stars.[2]

In a very short period of time, our understanding of the universe changed forever.

Today we can see some of these distant galaxies.[3]

We know that they are there.

They have been there for a very long time.

But before mankind had instruments powerful enough to gather celestial light and bring these galaxies into visibility, we did not believe such a thing was possible.

The immensity of the universe didn't suddenly change, but our ability to see and understand this truth changed dramatically. And with that greater light, mankind was introduced to glorious vistas we had never before imagined.

IT IS HARD FOR US TO BELIEVE WHAT WE CANNOT SEE

Suppose you were able to travel back in time and have a conversation with people who lived a thousand or even a hundred years ago. Imagine trying to describe to them some of the modern technologies that you and I take for granted today. For example, what might these people think of us if we told them stories of jumbo jets, microwave ovens, handheld devices that contain vast digital libraries, and videos of our grandchildren that we instantly share with millions of people around the world?

Some might believe us. Most would ridicule, oppose, or perhaps even seek to silence or harm us. Some might attempt to apply logic, reason, and facts as they know them to show that we are misguided, foolish, or even dangerous. They might condemn us for attempting to mislead others.

But of course, these people would be completely mistaken. They might be well-meaning and sincere. They might feel absolutely positive of their opinion. But they simply would not be able to see clearly because they had not yet received the more complete light of truth.

It seems to be a trait of humanity to assume that we are right even when we are wrong. And if that is the case, what hope is there for any of us? Are we destined to drift aimlessly on an ocean of conflicting information, stranded on a raft we have poorly pieced together from our own biases?

Is it possible to find truth?

Yes! The joyful message is that God Himself—the Lord of Hosts who knows all truth—has given His children the promise that they can know truth for themselves.

God cares about you. He will listen, and He will answer your personal questions. The answers to your prayers will come in His own way and in His own time, and therefore, you need to learn to listen to His voice. God wants you to find your way back to Him, and the Savior is the way (see John 14:6). God wants you to learn of His Son, Jesus Christ, and experience the profound peace and joy that come from following the path of divine discipleship.

My dear friends, here is a fairly straightforward experiment, with a guarantee from God, found in a book of ancient scripture available to every man, woman, and child willing to put it to the test:

First, you must search the word of God. That means reading the scriptures and studying the words of the ancient as well as modern prophets regarding the restored gospel of Jesus Christ—not with an intent to doubt or criticize but with a sincere desire to discover truth. Ponder upon the things you will feel, and prepare your minds to receive the truth (see 3 Ne. 17:3).

Second, you must consider, ponder, fearlessly strive to believe (see D&C 67:3), and be grateful for how merciful the Lord has been to His children from the time of Adam to our day by providing prophets, seers, and revelators to lead His Church and help us find the way back to Him.

Third, you must ask your Heavenly Father, in the name of His Son, Jesus Christ, to manifest the truth of The Church of Jesus Christ of Latter-day Saints unto you. Ask with a sincere heart and with real intent, having faith in Christ (see Moro. 10:3–5).

There is also a *fourth* step. When you are trying to verify the truth of gospel principles, you must first live them. Put gospel doctrine and Church teachings to the test in your own life. Do it with real intent and enduring faith in God.

If you will do these things, you have a promise from God—who is bound by His word (see D&C 82:10)—that He will manifest the truth to you by the power of the Holy Ghost. He will grant you greater light that will allow you to look through the darkness and witness unimaginably glorious vistas incomprehensible to mortal sight.

The more we incline our hearts and minds toward God, the more heavenly light distills upon our souls. And each time we willingly and earnestly seek that light, we indicate to God our readiness to receive more light. Gradually, things that before seemed hazy, dark, and remote become clear, bright, and familiar to us.

In the end, we are all pilgrims seeking God's light as we journey on the path of discipleship. We do not condemn others for the amount of light they may or may not have; rather, we nourish and encourage all light until it grows clear, bright, and true.

Let us acknowledge that most often gaining a testimony is not a task of a minute, an hour, or a day. It is not once and done. The process of gathering spiritual light is the quest of a lifetime.

Your testimony of the living Son of God and His restored Church, The Church of Jesus Christ of Latter-day Saints, may not come as quickly as you desire, but I promise you this: if you do your part, it will come.

And it will be glorious.

FOCUS ON WHAT
MATTERS MOST

On a dark December night in 1972, a Lockheed 1011 jumbo jet crashed into the Florida Everglades, killing over 100 people. This terrible accident was one of the deadliest crashes in the history of the United States.

A curious thing about this accident is that all vital parts and systems of the airplane were functioning perfectly—the plane could have easily landed safely at its destination in Miami, only twenty miles (thirty-two kilometers) away.

During the final approach, however, the crew noticed that one green light had failed to illuminate—a light that indicates whether or not the nose landing gear has extended successfully. The pilots discontinued the approach, set the aircraft into a circling holding pattern over the pitch-black Everglades, and turned their attention toward investigating the problem.

They became so preoccupied with their search that they failed to realize the plane was gradually descending closer and closer toward the dark swamp below. By the time someone noticed what was happening, it was too late to avoid the disaster.

After the accident, investigators tried to determine the cause. The landing gear had indeed lowered properly. The plane was in perfect mechanical condition. Everything was working properly—all except one thing: a single burned-out lightbulb. That tiny bulb—worth about twenty cents—started the chain of events that ultimately led to the tragic death of over 100 people.

Of course, the malfunctioning lightbulb didn't cause the accident; it happened because the crew placed its focus on something that seemed to matter at the moment while losing sight of what mattered most.

The tendency to focus on the insignificant at the expense of the profound happens not only to pilots but to everyone. We are all at risk. The driver who focuses on the road has a far greater chance of arriving at his destination accident-free than the driver who focuses on sending text messages on his phone.

We know what matters most in life—the Light of Christ teaches this to everyone. We as faithful Latter-day Saints have the Holy Ghost as a "constant companion" to teach us the things of eternal value (D&C 121:46).

We cannot and must not allow ourselves to get distracted from focusing on our sacred duties—serving God and loving our fellowmen. We cannot and we must not lose focus on these things that matter most.

USE TIME WISELY

In reality, time is perhaps the only commodity of life that is divided equally among every person in the world. Think about it—we all have twenty-four hours in a day. Though some people have more demands on their time than others, we all have an equal opportunity to use those twenty-four hours wisely.

I learned how remarkably fairly time is distributed while on long-range flights around the world. For example, we departed Frankfurt at 10:00 a.m. local time and, after an eleven-hour flight in a B-747, arrived in San Francisco at 12:00 noon California time, apparently only two hours later. That was wonderful—we had gained nine hours! Of course, you all know, on the next day, on our way back to Frankfurt, we lost the nine hours again.

Someone has said, "Time cannot be expanded, accumulated, mortgaged, hastened, or retarded."[1]

And it is ever renewing. Even though we may have wasted time yesterday, there is hope. There is a full day waiting for us today and tomorrow.

AS ELDER NEAL A. MAXWELL PUT IT:

"Either we use time wisely or it uses us; either we manage tasks effectively, or we are pushed about and prodded by them."[2]

RIGHTEOUS MOTIVES

Let me share with you a personal experience from my own youth about the power of righteous motives.

After the turmoil of the Second World War, my family ended up in Russian-occupied East Germany. When I attended fourth grade I had to learn Russian. I found this quite difficult because of the Cyrillic alphabet, but as time went on I seemed to do all right.

When I turned eleven we had to leave East Germany overnight because of the political orientation of my father. I began going to school in West Germany, which was American-occupied at that time. In school there, all children were required to learn English, not Russian. To learn Russian had been difficult, but English was impossible for me. I thought my mouth was not made for speaking English. My teachers struggled. My parents suffered. And I knew English was definitely not my language.

But then something changed in my young life. As often as I could, I rode my bicycle to the airport and watched airplanes take off and land. I read, studied, and learned everything I could find about aviation. It was my greatest desire to become a pilot. I could already picture myself in the cockpit of an airliner or in a military fighter plane. I felt deep in my heart this was what I should pursue in life!

Then I learned that to become a pilot I needed to speak English. Overnight, to the total surprise of everybody, it appeared as if my mouth had changed. It still took a lot of work, persistence, and patience, but I was able to learn English!

Why? Because of a righteous and strong motive!

Our motives and thoughts ultimately influence our actions.

Webb Air Force Base, Texas, 1961.

The testimony of the truthfulness of the restored gospel of Jesus Christ is the most powerful motivating force in our lives. Jesus repeatedly emphasized the power of good thoughts and proper motives: "Look unto me in every thought; doubt not, fear not" (D&C 6:36).

The testimony of Jesus Christ and the restored gospel will help us in our lives to learn of God's specific plan for us and then to act accordingly. It gives us assurance of the reality, truth, and goodness of God, of the teachings and Atonement of Jesus Christ, and of the divine calling of latter-day prophets. Our testimony motivates us to live righteously, and righteous living will cause our testimony to grow stronger.

TOOLS IN THE HANDS OF GOD

I once owned a pen that I loved to use during my career as an airline captain. By simply turning the shaft, I could choose one of four colors. The pen did not complain when I wanted to use red ink instead of blue. It did not say to me, "I would rather not write after 10:00 p.m., in heavy fog, or at high altitudes." The pen did not say, "Use me only for important documents, not for the daily, mundane tasks." With greatest reliability it performed every task I needed, no matter how important or insignificant. It was always ready to serve.

In a similar way we are tools in the hands of God. When our heart is in the right place, we do not complain that our assigned task is unworthy of our abilities. We gladly serve wherever we are asked. When we do this, the Lord can use us in ways beyond our own understanding to accomplish His work.

JOY IN CHURCH SERVICE

Many years ago a couple of fellow airline captains and I decided to fulfill a boyhood dream of restoring an antique airplane. Together we purchased a worn-down 1938 Piper Cub and started the work of returning it to its original form. The project was a labor of love. It had special meaning for me because I had learned to fly in a similar airplane when I was a young man.

This airplane was built only thirty-five years after the Wright brothers made their famous first flight. Just thinking of that makes me feel grateful to have lived in these times of exploration and invention.

The engine of our Piper Cub did not have an electric starter; as you were priming the engine from the cockpit, someone else on the ground would grab hold of the propeller and hurl it with might until the engine would run on its own. Each engine start was a moment of excitement and bravery.

Once the plane was airborne, it became clear the Piper Cub was not built for speed. As a matter of fact, when there was a strong headwind, it seemed as though we were not moving at all. I remember flying together with my teenage

Lt Mark Tedrow   Lcdr Todd Royles

son, Guido, above the autobahn in Germany, and sure enough, the cars below passed us comfortably!

But, oh, how I loved this little plane! It was the perfect way to experience the wonder and beauty of flight. You could hear, feel, smell, taste, and see what flying was all about. The Wright brothers expressed it this way: "There is [nothing] equal to that which aviators enjoy while being carried through the air on great white wings."[1]

In contrast, more recently I had the privilege to fly in a sophisticated F-18 fighter jet with the world-famous Blue Angels, the United States Navy's flight demonstration team. It was like taking a flight above and along memory lane because exactly fifty years before, almost to the day, I had completed my training as an Air Force fighter pilot.

The F-18 flight experience, of course, was totally different from the one in the Piper Cub. It was like applying the existing laws of aerodynamics in a more perfect way. However, flying with the Blue Angels also quickly reminded me that being a jet fighter pilot is a young man's game. To quote the Wright brothers again, "More than anything else the sensation [of flying] is one of perfect peace, mingled with an excitement that strains every nerve to the utmost."[2] In addition, flying with the Blue Angels suggested a totally different way of having "angels" round about you and bearing you up.

If you were to ask me which of these two flying experiences I enjoyed more, I'm not sure I could tell you. In some obvious ways, they were very different, to say the least. And yet in other ways, they were very much the same.

In both the Piper Cub and the F-18, I felt the excitement, beauty, and joy of flight. In both I could feel the call of the poet to "[slip] the surly bonds of Earth and [dance] the skies on laughter-silvered wings."[3]

Now, you might ask, what do these two totally different flying experiences have to do with serving in this Church we all love so much?

Isn't it true that our individual experiences of service may all be quite different? We could say some of you are flying in F-18 jets, while others are flying in Piper Cubs. Some of you live in wards and stakes where every position is filled with an active member. Yours is the privilege to participate in a ward organization that is well staffed.

Others of you live in areas of the world where there is only a small handful of Church members. You may feel alone and burdened with the weight of all that needs to be done. For you it may take a lot of personal hands-on involvement to get the engine of Church service started. Sometimes it may even seem that your branch or ward is not moving forward at all.

However, no matter what your responsibilities or circumstances may be, you and I know there is always a special joy that comes from dedicated service.

I always loved flying, whether it was in a Piper Cub, an F-18, or any other plane. While in the Piper Cub, I did not complain about the lack of speed; while in the F-18, I did not grumble when the strain of the aerobatic maneuvers mercilessly revealed the realities of my advancing age.

Yes, there is always something imperfect in any situation. Yes, it is easy to find things to complain about.

But whether in a large ward or a small branch, we are all called upon to serve, to bless, and to act in all things for the good of everyone and everything entrusted to our care. Could there be anything more exhilarating?

During my career as an airline pilot, I had the opportunity to be a check and training captain. Part of this job was to train and test experienced pilots to ensure that they had the necessary knowledge and skills to safely and efficiently operate those magnificent big jets.

I found that there were pilots who, even after many years of flying professionally, never lost the thrill of climbing into the atmosphere. They loved the sound of rushing air, the growling of the powerful engines, the feeling of being "one with the wind and one with the dark sky and the stars ahead."[4] Their enthusiasm was contagious.

There were also a few who seemed to be merely going through the motions. They had mastered the systems and the handling of the jets, but somewhere along the way they had lost the joy of flying "where never lark, or even eagle flew."[5] They had lost their sense of awe at a glowing sunrise, at the beauties of God's creations as they crossed oceans and continents. If they met the official requirements, I certified them, but at the same time I felt sorry for them.

You may want to ask yourself if you are merely going through the motions as a member of the Church—doing what is expected but not experiencing the joy that should be yours. Serving in the Church gives us abundant opportunities to feel the joy that Ammon expressed: "Have we not great reason to rejoice? . . . We have been instruments in [the Lord's] hands of doing this great and marvelous work. Therefore, let us glory . . . in the Lord; yea, we will rejoice" (Alma 26:13, 15–16).

Our religion is a joyful one! In the book of Psalms we read, "Blessed is the people that know the joyful sound: they shall walk, O Lord, in the light of thy countenance" (Ps. 89:15). We can experience this greater joy if we but look for it.

Too often we fail to experience the bliss that comes from daily, practical service. At times assignments can feel like burdens.

Let us not pass through life immersed in the three **W**s:

WEARIED,

WORRYING,

and **WHINING.**

We live beneath our privileges when we allow worldly anchors to keep us away from the abundant joy that comes from faithful and dedicated service, especially within the walls of our own homes.

We live beneath our privileges when we fail to partake of the feast of happiness, peace, and joy that God grants so bountifully to His faithful servants.

My dear friends, may we diligently seek to learn the doctrine of the gospel, may we strengthen our testimonies line upon line by receiving the revelations of the Spirit, and may we find true joy in daily service. As we do these things, we will begin to live up to our potential and privileges and we will be able to "do all things through Christ which strengtheneth [us]" (Philip. 4:13).

THE HOLY GHOST:
OUR POLAR STAR

In piloting an airplane, you learn quickly that your flight path depends greatly on how you handle challenging external influences such as wind and weather. Even more important, however, are the decisions you make in response to those external influences. Your decisions, in fact, can counteract the external influences to ensure that you stay on course and reach your desired eternal, divine destination. In order to make those decisions correctly, it helps to know what your actual position is. Therefore, it is of vital importance to have a true and valid reference point like the polar star in the Northern Hemisphere or a reliable electronic platform wherever you are.

As you know, there are plenty of winds and storms in the world today that attempt to blow you off course. In order to continue the course you have begun, you need a spiritual polar star in your life. You need a point of reference that has eternal consistency and reliability.

I bear witness to you, individually and collectively, that you do have the most stable and dependable reference platform for your spiritual and physical position available to you. It will help you to know at all times and in all places whether or not you are on the right path.

It is the companionship of the Holy Ghost. Therefore, always be worthy of the companionship of the Holy Ghost.

Do nothing without the Spirit of God. The presence of the Spirit of God will bring focus, certainty, and confidence into your life. And "by the power of the Holy Ghost [you] may know the truth of all things" (Moro. 10:5). The gift and the power of "the Holy Ghost . . . will show unto you all things what [you] should do" (2 Ne. 32:5).

What a wonderful promise for you as you move forward into your future.

WEATHERING THE
TURBULENCE

DO YOUR BEST

In the 1960s I attended pilot training in the United States Air Force. I was far away from my home, a young West German soldier, born in Czechoslovakia, who had grown up in East Germany and spoke English only with great difficulty. I clearly remember my journey to our training base in Texas. It was a commercial flight from Newark, New Jersey, to San Antonio, Texas, in a beautiful Lockheed Super Constellation. I was sitting next to a passenger who spoke with a heavy Southern accent. I could scarcely understand a word he said. I actually wondered if I had been taught the wrong language all along. I was terrified by the thought that I had to compete for the coveted top spots in pilot training against students who were native English speakers. Fortunately, we were given additional language training at Lackland Air Force Base in San Antonio.

When I finally arrived on our jet training base in the small town of Big Spring, Texas, one of the first things I did was to look for the Latter-day Saint branch. It consisted of a handful of wonderful members who were meeting in rented rooms on the air base itself. The members were in the process of building a small

Earning my wings in Big Spring, Texas, 1962.

meetinghouse that would serve as a permanent place for the Church. Back in those days members provided much of the labor on new buildings.

Day after day I attended my pilot training and studied as hard as I could and then spent most of my spare time working on the new meetinghouse. There I learned that a two-by-four is not a dance step but a piece of wood. I also learned the important survival skill of missing my thumb when pounding a nail.

I spent so much time working on the meeting-house that the branch president—who also happened to be one of our flight instructors—expressed concern that I perhaps should spend more time studying.

My friends and fellow student pilots who were not members of the Church engaged themselves in free-time activities as well, although I think it's safe to say that some of those activities would not have been in alignment with today's *For the Strength of Youth* pamphlet. For my part, I enjoyed being an active part of this tiny West Texas branch, practicing my newly acquired carpentry skills, and improving my English as I fulfilled my callings to teach in the elders quorum and in Sunday School.

At the time, Big Spring, despite its name, was a small, insignificant, and unknown place. And I often felt exactly the same way about myself—insignificant, unknown, and quite alone. Even so, I never once wondered if the Lord had forgotten me or if He would ever be able to find me there. I knew that it didn't matter to Heavenly Father where I was, where I ranked in performance with others in my pilot training class, or what my calling in the Church was.

What mattered to Him was that I was doing the best I could, that my heart was inclined toward Him, and that I was willing to help those around me. I knew if I did the best I could, all would be well.

And all was well.[1]

THE DIFFERENCE OF
A FEW DEGREES

In 1979, a large passenger jet with 257 people on board left New Zealand for a sightseeing flight to Antarctica and back. Unknown to the pilots, however, someone had modified the flight coordinates by a mere two degrees. This error placed the aircraft twenty-eight miles (forty-five kilometers) to the east of where the pilots assumed they were. As they approached Antarctica, the pilots descended below the minimum safe altitude to give the passengers a better look at the landscape. Although both were experienced pilots, neither had made this particular flight before, and they had no way of knowing that the incorrect coordinates had placed them directly in the path of Mount Erebus, an active volcano that rises from the frozen landscape to a height of more than 12,000 feet (3,700 meters).

As the pilots flew onward, the white of the snow and ice covering the volcano blended with the white of the clouds above, making it appear as though they were flying over flat ground. By the time the instruments sounded the warning that the ground was rising fast toward them, it was too late. The airplane crashed into the side of the volcano, killing everyone on board.

It was a terrible tragedy initiated by a minor error—a matter of only a few degrees.[1]

Through years of serving the Lord and in countless interviews, I have learned that the difference between happiness and misery in individuals, in marriages, and families often comes down to an error of only a few degrees.

SAUL, THE KING OF ISRAEL

The story of Saul, the king of Israel, illustrates this point. Saul's life began with great promise, but it had an unfortunate and tragic end. In the beginning, Saul was "a choice young man, . . . and there was not among the children of Israel a goodlier person than he" (1 Sam. 9:2). Saul was personally chosen by God to be king.[2] He had every advantage—he was physically imposing,[3] and he came from an influential family.[4]

Of course, Saul had weaknesses, but the Lord promised to bless, uphold, and prosper him. The scriptures tell us that God promised to always be with him,[5] give him another heart,[6] and turn him into another man.[7]

When he had the Lord's help, Saul was a magnificent king. He united Israel and defeated the Ammonites, who had invaded their land.[8] Soon a much greater problem faced him—the Philistines, who had a terrible army with chariots and horsemen "and people as the sand which is on the sea shore in multitude"

(1 Sam. 13:5). The Israelites were so terrified of the Philistines that they hid "themselves in caves, and in thickets, and in rocks" (1 Sam. 13:6).

The young king needed help. The prophet Samuel sent word for Saul to wait for him to come and offer sacrifice and seek counsel from the Lord. Saul waited seven days, and still the prophet Samuel had not arrived. Finally, Saul felt he could wait no longer. He gathered the people together and did something he had no priesthood authority to do—he offered the sacrifice himself.

When Samuel arrived, he was brokenhearted. "Thou hast done foolishly," he said. If only the new king had endured a little longer and not deviated from the course of the Lord, if only he had followed the revealed order of the priesthood, the Lord would have established his kingdom forever. "But now," Samuel said, "thy kingdom shall not continue" (1 Sam. 13:13–14).

On that day, the prophet Samuel recognized a critical weakness in Saul's character. When pressured by outside influences, Saul did not have the self-discipline to stay on course, trust the Lord and His prophet, and follow the pattern God had established.

SMALL ERRORS CAN HAVE A LARGE IMPACT ON OUR LIVES

The difference of a few degrees, as with the Antarctica flight or Saul's failure to hold fast to the counsel of the prophet just a little longer, may seem minor. But even small errors over time can make a dramatic difference in our lives.

Let me share with you how I taught the same principle to young pilots.

Suppose you were to take off from an airport at the equator, intending to circumnavigate the globe, but your course was off by just one degree. By the time you returned to the same longitude, how far off course would you be? A few miles? A hundred miles? The answer might surprise you. An error of only one degree would put you almost 500 miles (800 kilometers) off course, or one hour of flight for a jet plane.

No one wants his life to end in tragedy. But all too often, like the pilots and passengers of the sightseeing flight, we set out on what we hope will be an exciting journey only to realize too late that an error of a few degrees has set us on a course for spiritual disaster.

IS THERE A LESSON FOR OUR LIVES IN THESE EXAMPLES?

Small errors and minor drifts away from the doctrine of the gospel of Jesus Christ can bring sorrowful consequences into our lives. It is therefore of critical importance that we become self-disciplined enough to make early and decisive corrections to get back on the right track and not wait or hope that errors will somehow correct themselves.

The Lord reminds us that "unto whom much is given much is required" (D&C 82:3). May we courageously follow the promptings of the Holy Ghost to make decisive and timely corrections that will bring us back on course.

TURN AWAY FROM TEMPTATION

Several years ago, President Thomas S. Monson and I were offered an opportunity to tour Air Force One—the magnificent aircraft that transports the President of the United States. There were painstaking security checks by the Secret Service, and I smiled a little as agents searched our dear prophet prior to boarding.

Then the pilot in command guided us to the cockpit and invited me to take the captain's seat. It was a remarkable experience to again sit at the helm of a wonderful flying machine like the kind I had flown for so many years. Memories of flights across oceans and continents flooded my heart and mind. I envisioned exciting takeoffs and landings at airports all over the world.

Almost unconsciously, and as I have done so often to begin the takeoff roll, I placed my hands on the four throttles of the 747. Just then, a beloved and unmistakable voice came from behind—the voice of Thomas S. Monson.

"Dieter," he said, "don't even think about it."

I'm not admitting to anything, but it just may be that President Monson read my mind.

When we are tempted to do things we should not do, let us listen to the loving warning voices of trusted family, friends, Church leaders, our beloved prophet, the still small voice, and always the Savior.

MINIMIZE THE EFFECTS
OF TURBULENCE

It's remarkable how much we can learn about life by studying nature. For example, scientists can look at the rings of trees and make educated guesses about climate and growing conditions hundreds and even thousands of years ago. One of the things we learn from studying the growth of trees is that during seasons when conditions are ideal, trees grow at a normal rate. However, during seasons when growing conditions are not ideal, trees slow down their growth and devote their energy to the basic elements necessary for survival.

At this point some of you may be thinking, "That's all very fine and good, but what does it have to do with flying an airplane?" Well, let me tell you.

Have you ever been in an airplane and experienced turbulence? The most common cause of turbulence is a sudden change in speed or direction of air movement causing the aircraft to pitch, yaw, and roll. While planes are built to easily withstand far greater turbulence than anything you would ever encounter on a regular flight, turbulence still may be quite disconcerting to passengers.

What do you suppose pilots do when they encounter turbulence? A student pilot may think that increasing speed is a good strategy because it will get them through the turbulence faster. But that may be the wrong thing to do. Professional pilots understand that there is an optimum turbulence penetration speed that will minimize the negative effects of turbulence. And most of the time that would mean to reduce your speed. The same principle applies to cars as they cross over speed bumps on a road.

Therefore, it is good advice, even for normal life challenges to slow down a little, steady the course, and focus on the essentials when experiencing adverse conditions.

DISTRESS AND THE IMPORTANCE OF HOPE

Just as every pilot will encounter turbulence at some point in his or her career, all of us will experience calamity during our lives. Occasionally, despite our faith and preparation, aircraft engines fail and powerful storms damage sensitive navigational instruments.

When catastrophe strikes, it can seem nearly impossible for us to avoid feeling overwhelmed by emotions of suffering, sorrow, helplessness, and anger. These feelings are natural and should not be ignored or carelessly dismissed. The Old Testament reminds us, "To every thing there is a season, and a time to every purpose under the heaven: . . . A time to weep, and a time to laugh; a time to mourn, and a time to dance; . . . A time to love, and a time to hate; a time of war, and a time of peace" (Eccl. 3:1, 4, 8).

Lufthansa Chief Pilot, 1982, in the cockpit of a DC10.

Although becoming a pilot had been my dream, once I achieved my goal I continued to face challenges and times of great difficulty. One such occasion occurred in December of 1973. It tested every person involved.

A group of armed men invaded the Fiumicino Airport in Rome, Italy, captured an airplane, and detonated explosive devices, resulting in the deaths of dozens of people on board. Five men then took several hostages and hijacked a Lufthansa Boeing 737 scheduled to depart for Munich, Germany.

The plane, which contained the captain, first officer, two flight attendants, two members of the ground crew, and eight additional hostages, took off for Athens, Greece, on the orders of these five men.

When we received word of the attack and hijacking, Lufthansa assigned me, as a chief pilot of the B-737 fleet, to follow the hijacked plane wherever these men might take it. Our team used all of the resources and professional tricks at our disposal to help our crew and the rest of the hostages, all the while praying that the hijackers would not hurt any more innocent people.

Unfortunately, one additional hostage was killed while the hijacked plane was in Athens. There was nothing we could do about it. The ordeal continued as the aircraft took off and approached several different countries, each time making demands of the local governments. Eventually, with the help and intervention of many good people, the B-737 was allowed to finally land in Kuwait, and the hostages were released. What a relief it was when I was able to fly the hijacked plane back to Germany, knowing that the crew and the rest of the hostages could feel safe now.

Feelings of anxiety, helplessness, and anger as we searched for solutions were replaced by relief, happiness, gratitude, and hope for healing as we were flying the battered aircraft back to our home airport and to safety.

In this life it can seem that injustice is the rule rather than the exception. There are "wars, rumors of wars, and earthquakes in divers places . . . great pollutions upon the face of the earth; . . . murders, and robbing" (Morm. 8:30–31). When we or those we love are afflicted by misfortune or the poor decisions of others, we may be tempted to become bitter.

While there is a "time to mourn," there is also "a time to heal." It is through the Atonement of Jesus Christ that we can find healing and "peace in this world, and eternal life in the world to come" (D&C 59:23). It is through His love and our love for Him that we can learn to be grateful in any circumstance.

Being grateful in times of distress does not mean that we are pleased with our circumstances. It does mean that through the eyes of faith we look beyond our present-day challenges.

THIS IS NOT A GRATITUDE OF THE LIPS BUT OF THE SOUL. IT IS A GRATITUDE

THAT HEALS THE HEART AND EXPANDS THE MIND. BECAUSE THIS

KIND OF GRATITUDE IS ROOTED IN FAITH IN OUR SAVIOR, IT

INSPIRES HUMILITY AND FOSTERS EMPATHY TOWARD

OUR FELLOWMEN AND ALL OF GOD'S CREATION.

AVOID THE STORM

On my flights from Europe to Africa I often could observe the interesting weather phenomenon called the intertropical convergence zone. In simple terms, it is a band of thunderstorms that moves north and south across the equator, filling the horizon with billowing, menacing columns of clouds.

I could scarcely look at these clouds without being fascinated with their beauty and majesty. They towered in massive black formations, and within them lightning sparked with brilliant light from one end to the other in an indescribable fury of fire. What a glorious and fascinating sight!

But what do you think pilots do when they approach these storms? They do everything in their power to avoid them—no matter how beautiful and intriguing those thunderstorms appear. As moisture rises in the clouds, it begins to freeze, forming hail the size of soccer balls that can puncture metal and destroy an aircraft. When flying through those clouds, ice, severe turbulence, and electric discharges can cripple the airplane and its systems.

Isn't the same principle true when you see things that could cause spiritual harm?

TEMPTATION WOULDN'T BE TEMPTATION IF IT DIDN'T APPEAR ATTRACTIVE, FASCINATING, OR FUN. BUT, LIKE THE PILOT APPROACHING A STORM, YOU NEED TO LEARN TO AVOID IT, NO MATTER HOW BEAUTIFUL OR INTRIGUING IT MAY APPEAR FROM THE OUTSIDE.

Because Heavenly Father loves His children, He has given us the commandments to keep us at a safe distance from those harmful storms. He does not force any of His children to walk in His way. He allows and expects us to choose for ourselves. But know this: some choices may lead to disaster. Avoid disaster, choose wisely, choose the right.

I add my witness to the chorus of warnings against the terrible problem of pornography. Steer clear of it. Stay away from it. The same words we use to train pilots regarding destructive thunderstorms apply to you regarding pornography: "Avoid, avoid, avoid!"

Don't assume that you can put the nose of the airplane just a little bit inside the storm—do not flirt with pornography. Remember that often the most disgusting and destructive of things can appear attractive in the beginning or from the outside. Steer clear of things that can endanger your worthiness, marriage, or happiness in this life and in the life to come.

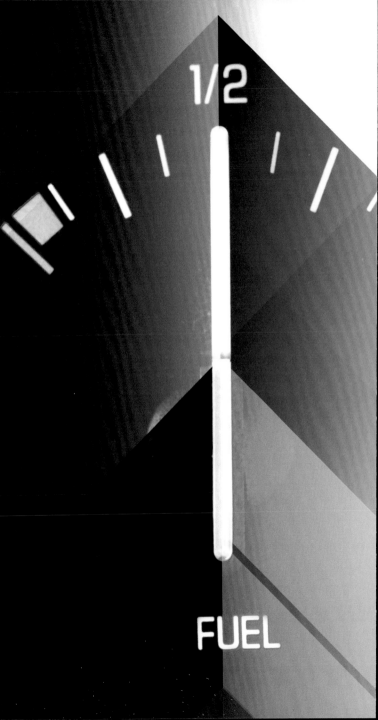

POINT OF SAFE RETURN

During my training to become an airline captain, I had to learn how to navigate an airplane over long distances. Flights over huge oceans, crossing extensive deserts, and connecting continents need careful planning to ensure a safe arrival at the planned destination. Some of these nonstop flights can last beyond fourteen hours and cover more than 9,000 miles.

There is an important decision point during such long flights commonly known as the point of safe return. Up to this point the aircraft has enough fuel to turn around and return safely to the airport of departure. Having passed the point of safe return, the captain has lost this option and has to continue on. That is why this point is often referred to as the point of no return.

Satan, "the father of all lies" (2 Ne. 2:18), "the father of contention" (3 Ne. 11:29), "the author of all sin" (Hel. 6:30), and the "enemy unto God" (Moro. 7:12), uses the forces of evil to convince us that this concept applies whenever we have sinned. The scriptures call him the "accuser" because he wants us to feel that we are beyond forgiveness (see Rev. 12:10).

Satan wants us to think that when we have sinned we have gone past a "point of safe return"—that it is too late to change our course.

In our beautiful but also troubled world, it is a sad reality that this attitude is the source of great sorrow, grief, and distress to families, marriages, and individuals.

Satan tries to counterfeit the work of God, and by doing this he may deceive many. To make us lose hope, feel miserable like himself, and believe that we are beyond forgiveness, Satan might even misuse words from the scriptures that emphasize the justice of God, in order to imply that there is no mercy.

The gift and sacrifice of our Savior guarantees that there never needs to be a "point of no return" in our spiritual life. Our loving Heavenly Father offered His Son to always keep open the gate for a safe return if we only walk through it by using true repentance and receiving the miracle of forgiveness.

OUR ETERNAL
DESTINATION

SEE THE END FROM
THE BEGINNING

Allow me to share with you an experience from my own boyhood. When I was eleven years old, my family had to leave East Germany and begin a new life in West Germany overnight. Until my father could get back into his original profession as a government employee, my parents operated a small laundry business in our little town. I became the laundry delivery boy. To be able to do that effectively, I needed a bicycle to pull the heavy laundry cart. I had always dreamed of owning a nice, sleek, shiny, sporty red bicycle. But there had never been enough money to fulfill this dream. What I got instead was a heavy, ugly, black, sturdy workhorse of a bicycle. I delivered laundry on that bike before and after school for quite a few years. There were times when I was not overly excited about the bike, the cart, or my job. Sometimes the cart seemed so heavy and the work so tiring that I thought my lungs would burst, and I often had to stop to catch my breath. Nevertheless, I did my part because I knew we desperately needed the income as a family, and it was my way to contribute.

If I had only known back then what I learned many years later—if I had only been able to see the end from the beginning—I would have had a better appreciation of these experiences, and it would have made my job so much easier.

Many years later, when I was about to be drafted into the military, I decided to volunteer instead and join the air force to become a pilot. I loved flying and thought being a pilot would be my thing.

To be accepted for the program I had to pass a number of tests, including a number of very strict physical exams. The doctors were slightly concerned by some of the results and did some additional medical tests. Then they announced, "You have scars on your lung which are an indication of a lung disease in your early teenage years, but obviously you have healed now, and you qualify to enter the training program." The doctors asked me what kind of treatment I had gone through to heal the disease. Until the day of that examination I had not known that I had any kind of lung disease. Then it became clear to me that my regular exercise in fresh air as a laundry boy must have been a key factor in my healing from this illness. Without the extra effort of pedaling that heavy bicycle day in and day out, pulling the laundry cart up and down the streets of our town, I might never have become a jet fighter pilot and later a 747 airline captain.

We don't always know the details of our future. We do not know what lies ahead. We live in a time of uncertainty. We are surrounded by challenges on all sides. Occasionally discouragement may sneak into our day; frustration may invite itself into our thinking; doubt might enter about the value of our work. In these dark moments Satan whispers in our ears that we will never be able to succeed, that the price isn't worth the effort, and that our small part will never make a difference. He, the father of all lies, will try to prevent us from seeing the end from the beginning.

Fortunately, we are taught by the prophets, seers, and revelators of our day. How deeply grateful I am for the inspired leadership of the President of the Church, a living prophet of God for our time. His prophetic view helps us to see the end from the beginning.

I testify that if you trust the Lord and obey Him, His hand shall be over you. He will help you achieve the great potential He sees in you, and He will help you to see the end from the beginning.

PATIENCE WITH THE LORD'S TIMING

Every one of us is called to wait in our own way. We wait for answers to prayers and we wait for promised blessings. We wait for things which at the time may appear so right and so good that we can't possibly imagine why Heavenly Father would delay the answer or the blessing.

I remember very well the initial military phase of my training to become a fighter pilot. We spent a great part of our basic military training doing physical exercise. It was not just marching or strength training, but also running. I'm still not exactly sure why endless running was considered such an essential preparatory part of becoming a pilot. Nevertheless, we ran and we ran and we ran some more.

As I was running I began to notice something that, frankly, troubled me. Time and again I was being passed by my fellow cadets who smoked, drank, and did all manner of things that were contrary to the gospel and, in particular, to the Word of Wisdom.

I remember thinking, "Wait a minute! Aren't I supposed to be able to run and not be weary?" But I was weary, and I was overtaken by people who were definitely not following the Word of Wisdom. I confess, it troubled me at the time. I asked myself, was the scriptural promise true or was it not?

The answer didn't come immediately. But eventually I learned that God's promises are not always fulfilled as quickly as or in the exact way we might hope for; they come according to His timing and in His ways.

Years later I could see clear evidence of the temporal blessings that come to those who obey the Word of Wisdom—in addition to the spiritual blessings that come immediately from obedience to any of God's laws. The lessons we learn from patience will cultivate our character, lift our lives, and heighten our happiness. Looking back, I know for sure that the promises of the Lord, if perhaps not always swift, are always certain.

THE WORTH OF A SOUL

The more we learn about the universe, the more we understand—at least in a small part—what Moses knew. The universe is so large, mysterious, and glorious that it is incomprehensible to the human mind. "Worlds without number have I created," God said to Moses (Moses 1:33). The wonders of the night sky are a beautiful testimony of that truth.

There are few things that have filled me with such breathless awe as flying in the black of night across oceans and continents and looking out my cockpit window upon the infinite glory of millions of stars.

Astronomers have attempted to count the number of stars in the universe. One group of scientists estimates that the number of stars within range of our telescopes is ten times greater than all the grains of sand on the world's beaches and deserts.[1]

This conclusion has a striking similarity to the declaration of the ancient prophet Enoch: "Were it possible that man could number the particles of the earth, yea, millions of earths like this, it would not be a beginning to the number of thy creations" (Moses 7:30).

Given the vastness of God's creations, it's no wonder the great King Benjamin counseled his people to "always retain in remembrance, the greatness of God, and your own nothingness" (Mosiah 4:11).

But even though man is nothing, it fills me with wonder and awe to think that "the worth of souls is great in the sight of God" (D&C 18:10).

And while we may look at the vast expanse of the universe and say, "What is man in comparison to the glory of creation?" God Himself said we are the reason He created the universe! His work and glory—the purpose for this magnificent universe—is to save and exalt mankind (see Moses 1:38–39). In other words, the vast expanse of eternity, the glories and mysteries of infinite space and time are all built for the benefit of ordinary mortals like you and me. Our Heavenly Father created the universe that we might reach our potential as His sons and daughters.

This is a paradox of man: compared to God, man is nothing; yet we are everything to God. While against the backdrop of infinite creation we may appear to be nothing, we have a spark of eternal fire burning within our breast. We have the incomprehensible promise of exaltation—worlds without end—within our grasp. And it is God's great desire to help us reach it.

REACHING OUR DESTINATION

I spent many years in the cockpit of airplanes. During my commercial pilot career it was my task to safely get a big jet to our desired destination from any part of the world. To accomplish that I needed to keep in mind the big picture. It is so easy to be distracted often by unnecessary details. I knew with certainty that if I wanted to travel the most direct course from New York to Rome, I needed to fly east. If someone were to tell me that I should fly south, I knew there was no truth in his words. No amount of persuasion, no amount of flattery, bribery, or threats could convince me that flying south would get me to my destination, because I knew for myself.

WE ALL SEARCH FOR HAPPINESS, AND WE ALL TRY TO FIND OUR OWN "HAPPILY EVER AFTER." THE TRUTH IS, GOD KNOWS HOW TO GET THERE! AND HE HAS CREATED A MAP FOR US; HE KNOWS THE WAY.

He is our beloved Heavenly Father, who seeks our good, our happiness. He desires with all the love of a perfect and pure Father that we reach our supernal destination. The map is available to all. It gives explicit directions of what to do and where to go to everyone who is striving to come unto Christ and "stand as [a witness] of God at all times and in all things, and in all places" (Mosiah 18:9). All you have to do is trust your Heavenly Father. Trust Him enough to follow His plan.

Nevertheless, not all will follow the map. Some may look at it. Some may think it is reasonable, perhaps even true. But they do not follow the divine directions. Many believe that any road will take them to a "happily ever after." Some may even become angry when others who know the way try to help and assist them. They suppose that such advice is outdated, irrelevant, out of touch with modern life.

They suppose wrong.

I understand that, at times, some may wonder why they attend Church meetings or why it is so important to read the scriptures regularly or pray to our Heavenly Father daily. Here is my answer: we do these things because they are part of God's path for us. And that path will take us to our "happily ever after" destination.

We must also recognize that God has prepared a way that we can correct any misdirected navigation in this life and get back on course to Him and His Son. If we have chosen to fly south on our way to Rome, Heavenly Father, through His love and grace, has prepared a way that we still can reach our desired destination, if we only accept His guidance and follow it faithfully.

My dear friends—yes, all who stand for truth and righteousness, you who seek goodness and walk in the ways of the Lord—our Father in Heaven has promised that you will "mount up with wings as eagles; [you] shall run, and not be weary; and [you] shall walk, and not faint" (Isa. 40:31). You "shall not be deceived" (JS—M 1:37). God will bless and prosper you (see Mosiah 2:22–24). "The gates of hell shall not prevail against you; . . . and the Lord God will disperse the powers of darkness from before you, and cause the heavens to shake for your good, and his name's glory" (D&C 21:6).

As an Apostle of the Lord Jesus Christ, I leave you my blessing and give you a promise that as you accept and live the values and principles of the gospel of Jesus Christ, the day will come when you turn the final pages of your own glorious story; there you will read and experience the fulfillment of those blessed and wonderful words: "And they lived happily ever after."

NOTES

Taking Flight

1. See Tom D. Crouch, *The Bishop's Boys: A Life of Wilbur and Orville Wright* (New York: W. W. Norton, 1989), 166; see also lecture given by Wilbur Wright in Chicago on September 18, 1901, "Some Aeronautical Experiments," in *Journal of the Western Society of Engineers* (December 1901): 489–510, and in *The Papers of Wilbur and Orville Wright,* ed. Marvin W. McFarland (New York: McGraw-Hill, 1953), 1:99–118.

2. From Windsor Drawings 12282r., in *The Notebooks of Leonardo da Vinci* (Oxford and New York: Oxford University Press, 1980), 261.

3. *The Miracle of Forgiveness* (Salt Lake City: Bookcraft, 1969), 235.

4. *Nicomachean Ethics*, trans. W. D. Ross, book 3, chapter 5 (see Internet, http://classics.mit.edu/Aristotle/nicomachaen.3.iii.html).

5. *Key to the Science of Theology,* 5th ed. (Salt Lake City: George Q. Cannon and Sons, 1891), 102.

6. In Conference Report, Oct. 1961, 60–61.

7. *History of the Church*, 3:381.

Simplicity

1. Leonardo da Vinci, in John Cook, comp., *The Book of Positive Quotations*, 2nd ed. (1993), 262.

Light and Truth

1. See Marcia Bartusiak, *The Day We Found the Universe* (2009), xii. It is always surprising to me that we can be so confident of our conclusions. Sometimes our confidence is so great that we assume we have all the truth there is. Case in point: "Simon Newcomb, the dean of American astronomy in the late nineteenth century, remarked at an observatory dedication in 1887 that 'so far as astronomy is concerned . . . we do appear to be fast approaching the limits of our knowledge. . . . The result is that the work which really occupies the attention of the astronomer is less the discovery of new things than the elaboration of those already known'" (Bartusiak, xv).
2. It is interesting to consider Moses 1:33, 35 in light of this "recent" discovery. The book of Moses in the Pearl of Great Price was revealed to the Prophet Joseph Smith in June 1830, nearly a century before Edwin Hubble announced his discovery of distant galaxies.
3. See, for example, the Hubble Heritage Image Gallery at heritage.stsci.edu/gallery/gallery.html.

Use Time Wisely

1. Anonymous, in Cook, *The Book of Positive Quotations*, 274.
2. *The Smallest Part* (Salt Lake City: Deseret Book, 1973), 46.

Joy in Church Service

1. Wilbur Wright, in James Tobin, *To Conquer the Air: The Wright Brothers and the Great Race for Flight* (2003), 238.
2. Wright brothers, in Tobin, *To Conquer the Air,* 397.
3. John Gillespie Magee Jr., "High Flight," in Diane Ravitch, ed., *The American Reader: Words That Moved a Nation* (1990), 486.
4. Richard Bach, *Stranger to the Ground* (1963), 9.
5. Magee, "High Flight," 486.

Do Your Best

1. Dieter F. Uchtdorf graduated first in his class and received the coveted Commander's Trophy.

The Difference of a Few Degrees

1. See Arthur Marcel, "Mount Erebus Plane Crash," www.abc.net.au/rn/ockhamsrazor /stories/2007/1814952.htm.
2. See 1 Samuel 9:17.
3. See 1 Samuel 10:23.
4. See 1 Samuel 9:1.
5. See 1 Samuel 10:7.
6. See 1 Samuel 10:9.
7. See 1 Samuel 10:6.
8. See 1 Samuel 11:11.

The Worth of a Soul

1. See Andrew Craig, "Astronomers Count the Stars," *BBC News,* July 22, 2003, http:// news.bbc.co.uk/2/hi/science/nature/3085885.stm.

IMAGE CREDITS

ABOUT THE AUTHOR

President Dieter F. Uchtdorf has served in the First Presidency of The Church of Jesus Christ of Latter-day Saints since February 3, 2008. He was sustained as a member of the Quorum of the Twelve Apostles in October 2004. He became a General Authority in April 1994.

President Uchtdorf was born in 1940 in what is now the Czech Republic. He grew up in Zwickau, Germany, where his family joined the Church in 1947. He and his wife, Harriet Reich Uchtdorf, are the parents of two children and have six grandchildren and three great-grandchildren.

Prior to his calling as a General Authority, President Uchtdorf served six years in the German Air Force as a fighter pilot. He went on to become the senior vice president of flight operations and chief pilot of Lufthansa German Airlines.

Flying his desk, June 1990.